TRACING YOUR
FAMILY TREE

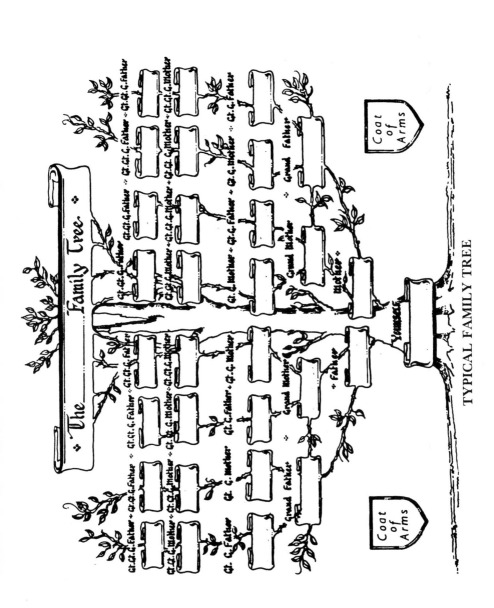

The _____ Family Tree.

Gt.Gt.Gt.G.Father ✦ Gt.Gt.G.Father ✦ Gt.Gt.G.Father ✦ Gt.Gt.G.Father
Gt.Gt.Gt.G.Mother ✦ Gt.Gt.G.Mother ✦ Gt.Gt.G.Mother ✦ Gt.Gt.G.Mother ✦ Gt.G.Father

Gt.G.Mother ✦ Gt.G.Father ✦ Gt.G.Mother ✦ Gt.G.Father

Grand Father

Grand Mother

Mother

Yourself

Coat of Arms

Gt.Gt.Gt.G.Father ✦ Gt.Gt.G.Father ✦ Gt.Gt.G.Father ✦ Gt.Gt.G.Father
Gt.Gt.Gt.G.Mother ✦ Gt.Gt.G.Mother ✦ Gt.G.G.Mother ✦ Gt.G.G.Mother

Gt.G.Father ✦ Gt.G.Mother

Grand Father

Grand Mother

Father

Coat of Arms

TYPICAL FAMILY TREE

TRACING YOUR FAMILY TREE

A Genealogical Guide

by

Victor J. Price

First published in April 1989 by
K.A.F. Brewin Books, Doric House,
Church Street, Studley, Warwickshire.

Reprinted September 1989.
Reprinted March 1991.
Reprinted October 1991.
Reprinted February 1996.
Reprinted July 2001.

ISBN 0 947731 50 4

Typeset in Baskerville
and printed and made in Great Britain
by Supaprint (Redditch) Ltd., Redditch, Worcs.

CONTENTS

ACKNOWLEDGEMENTS

Details of Sir Winston Churchill's Birth, Marriage and Death certificates are included by kind permission of His Grace, The Duke of Marlborough.

The design of the birth, marriage and death certificates shown is Crown copyright and is reproduced with the permission of Her Majesty's Stationery Office.

ILLUSTRATIONS

INTRODUCTION

There are 6 lessons on tracing your family history in this book, plus helpful details and respective information concerning your research.

It is a fascinating hobby, you may, from time to time, become frustrated and disappointed but you must be patient and persistent in your endeavours.

You should be able, without too much difficulty, to go back at least 4 to 5 generations. Do join your local Genealogy Society, for they have so much to offer you to help with your research and you will make many new friends.

VJP

'TO FORGET ONE'S ANCESTORS IS TO
BE A BROOK WITHOUT A SOURCE, A
TREE WITHOUT ROOTS'

LESSON No. 1

You must commence your enquiries from the known to the unknown.

Firstly question your parents and obtain from them as much information as you can as to their parentage, also check family bibles for entries.   Enter all the information obtained in a record book, also obtain copies of both your parents births and marriage certificates.   Then visit your grandparents, if they are still alive, from both sides of the family and obtain from them as much information as you can regarding their parents and relatives.   It is important to write down in a clear and authentic manner all the information obtained.

In the first instance it is recommended that you concentrate on your direct (or paternal) line i.e. your surname.

To illustrate, we will call you John Brown and give you two brothers, one older and one younger and a younger sister.   The older brother is named Wilfred, the younger Stanley and your younger sister is named Kate. You now have the first branch of your family tree.   Your father's name is Robert Brown and your mother's Barbara Kate Brown - nee Jackson.

Your father informs you that he has two brothers, Paul and Michael and two sisters, Susan and Barbara.   You now have the second branch of your family tree.

This will read as follows:-

2nd BRANCH.	Michael	Paul	Susan	Barbara	Robert Wilfred m	Barbara Kate Jackson.
	b 1930	b 1932	b 1934	b 1936	b 1938	b 1940
	d	d	d	d	d	d
						m 1959
1st BRANCH.		Wilfred	John	Stanley	Kate	
		b 1960	b 1962	b 1965	b 1970	

When the actual dates of births etc. are established these should be entered.

b = born. d = died. m = married. k = killed.

You now join each branch of your family tree with a vertical line.

From the details given you can deduct that your father married your mother when he was 21 years of age and she was aged 19 years.

LESSON No. 2

Your father now informs you that his father's name was Wilfred Brown and that he was killed in an accident at work in June 1950.   His mother's name was Margaret, maiden name Spencer, she died in August 1960, one year after he married your mother.   At that time the family resided in the Manchester area.   Birth, Marriage and Death Certificates relating to your grandparents had all now been lost.

Your course of action is now to obtain a copy of your grandfather's death certificate.   You can apply personally (or by post) to the Register Office of Births, Deaths and Marriages in Manchester.

The certificate will give you the following information:-

Registration District. County and year of death.

1	2	3	4	5	6
When and where died	Name and surname	Sex	Age	Occupation	Cause of death

7	8	9
Signature, description and residence of informant	When registered	Signature of registrar

Let us now assume that he died at the age of 50, this then establishes that he was born in 1900.   You now have to establish the actual date and place of birth. To do this you must attend, in person, to the offices of the General Register of Births, Deaths and Marriages in St. Catherine's House, 10 Kingsway, London WC2B 6JP.   The Public Search Rooms are open daily from 8.30 am to 4.30 pm Monday to Friday.   These offices are closed on public holidays. The main series of records maintained in these offices relate to **BIRTHS, DEATHS** and **MARRIAGES IN ENGLAND** and WALES from the 1st of JULY 1837 up to the present day.

The registers themselves are NOT open for inspection, the records are maintained quarterly in alphabetical order in indexes e.g. the birth index for March quarter, lists births registered in January, February and March, June quarter for April, May and June, and so on. These indexes can be searched free of charge. Each entry gives the Surname, Forename(s), Quarter, Year, District, Volume and Page No. following Volume No. It is imperative that you make an accurate note of these details for, if you apply for a full copy of the original certificate, these details must be entered on application form **PSR 1**, on parts A and B. It is the same system for searching for marriages and deaths but, forms **CAS 53** and **CAS 52** respectively have to be completed.

The completed forms then have to be taken to the cashiers office and the fee of £5.00 paid for each certificate required. These can be collected after 48 hours or posted to you free of charge. It will take several weeks before you receive these.

You now have the third branch of your family tree i.e.

3rd **BRANCH**	Wilfred m Margaret Spencer		
	b 1900	b ? ? ?	m -
	k June 1950	d August 1960	

LESSON No. 3

Let us now assume that you have received a copy of your grandfather's Birth Certificate from the General Register Office in London. This is most informative for it gives you not only his date of birth, 23 April 1900, but when and where he was born, his name, (if any) name and surname of both parents together with his mothers maiden name, occupation of his father, signature and description and residence of the informer and the date when registered. You are now in a position to compile the 4th branch of your family tree. Gt. Grandfathers name was Martin Brown and your Gt. Grandmothers name was Marjory Brown (nee Boswell).

4th BRANCH   <u>Martin m Marjory Boswell</u>

b	b		m
d	d		

You now have to do some assumptions as to the age of Martin and Marjory when they married. Let us assume that Martin was 20 at this stage as we are only interested in the paternal side of your family. From this we deduct that he was married around the year 1899.

A further visit to St. Catherine's House in London is now required and a search made of the marriage indexes. These are compiled in the same way as the Births (see lesson 2 para 5). When you have found the entry for a Martin Brown make a note of the registration details, your next move is to find the entry of marriage of Marjory Boswell, when you find this and the registration details agree you have found the correct marriage certificate.

5

You must remember that there could be twenty entered for a Martin Brown and you may have to go back several years before you find the correct entry. Patience is a virtue. In this case it would be better to first search for the marriage of Marjory Boswell as this surname is not as common as Brown, this would save you some time.

The certificate, when received, will give you the following information:-
Date when married. Names and surnames of both parties. Their ages. Condition i.e. Batchelor, Spinster, Widow etc. Rank or profession. Residence at time of marriage. Their fathers full names and rank or profession.

You now have the details for compiling the 5th branch of your family tree.

While checking the marriage indexes, why not check for the marriage of Wilfred Brown to Margret, the 3rd branch of your tree, you will then obtain her maiden name. As from 1911 onwards the marriage indexes shows, after the grooms entry i.e. Wilfred Brown, the brides surname, this does make your task much easier, follow the mentioned surname until you come across the one prefixed Marjory and, if the registration details tally you can then apply for a copy of the certificate, (if deemed necessary) with confidence.

Now is the time to continue back further with your family research as indicated in these lessons.

A note of warning, it should be pointed out that before 1875 failure to register bore no penalty and there may be some omissions in the Births register in particular; marriages and deaths were usually registered by the officiating clergyman or registrar after the ceremony.

All the indexes in St. Catherine's House from 1837 to 1865 are hand written, all entries are in strict alphabetical order. From 1866 they are printed. It is important to note that from this year (1866), in the DEATHS INDEX the age of the deceased is entered after the forename but, from the JUNE QUARTER in 1969 the date of birth is shown, if this is known, instead of the age. This is helpful in your research. It is useful to note that the place of death may not be the usual residence of the deceased, death may have occurred while visiting relatives or on holiday.

Regarding Birth Certifcates, it should be noted that

from September 1911 onwards the surname of the mother is entered immediately following the surname and fore-names of the child. If the mother's surname is known this can be a valuable check that the entry found is the correct one and could avoid the expense of applying for a full certificate. If the child was born out of wedlock, then the name of the father is not always shown and the child is registered under the surname of the mother, however, since 1875 the father's name may be inserted, in this case the birth is registered under both surnames.

In recent years the Births, Marriage and Death Indexes at St. Catherine's House in London have been filmed and copies deposited in the County Record Offices (CRO) in each of the Counties in England. You can go and check these, by appointment, and if you are successful in tracing the entries relating to your family, take note of the registration details and you can then apply, for a copy of the certificate required, by post to St. Catherine's House, but, if you do this each certificate will cost you £10.00. If you make a personal visit to St. Catherine's each certificate will only cost you £5.00.

If, for some reason you are not quite sure, that you have found the correct entry it is open to you, when completing the appropriate application forms, as applicable, to add additional details on the reverse side of the form. These further details are referred to as 'Checking Points'. Apply to the information desk for leaflet PSR 11, this will give you full details of this additional service. Should all the details given not prove that your application is the correct one you will receive a refund of £2.00 when personal application is made.

In addition to the system and layout explained in these three lessons, which only covers the paternal side of your family, (you can of course use this also for the maternal side), there are two alternatives i.e. Pedigree Chart and the Circular Diagram System, both these cover the paternal and maternal side of your family. (see illustrations).

Note: Since the 1st April 1991 the cost of copy certificates has been increased i.e.
Standard cert copy — £5.50, Short cert copy — £3.50.
If applied for at a Local Register Office or personally at St. Catherine's House in London.

These are copies of Birth, Marriage and Death Certificates to put you in the picture as to the contents of these documents.

These refer to the late Sir Winston Churchill who was Chancellor of the Exchequer, period 1924-1929, and Prime Minister of Great Britain during the years 1940-1945 and 1951-1955.

CERTIFIED COPY OF AN ENTRY OF BIRTH   GIVEN AT THE GENERAL REGISTER OFFICE, LONDON

Application Number 46·05·B.

REGISTRATION DISTRICT Woodstock

1874 BIRTH in the Sub-district of Woodstock in the County of Oxford

No.	When and where born	Name, if any	Sex	Name and surname of father	Name, surname and maiden surname of mother	Occupation of father	Signature, description and residence of informant	When registered	Signature of registrar	Name entered after registration
	Thirtieth November 1874 Blenheim	Winston Leonard	Boy	Randolph Henry Spencer Churchill	Jennie Churchill formerly Jerome	M.P. for Woodstock	Randolph S. Churchill father Blenheim	Twenty Sixth December 1874	George Register	

CERTIFIED to be a true copy of an entry in the certified copy of a Register of Births in the District above mentioned.
Given at the GENERAL REGISTER OFFICE, LONDON, under the Seal of the said Office, the 23rd day of November 1976

BXA 253978

CAUTION—Any person who (1) falsifies any of the particulars on this certificate, or (2) uses a falsified certificate as true, knowing it to be false, is liable to prosecution.

Form A 502M

CERTIFIED COPY OF AN ENTRY OF MARRIAGE   Given at the GENERAL REGISTER OFFICE, LONDON

Application Number 08·6·D

Registration District of St. George Hanover Square

1908. Marriage solemnized at The Parish Church
in the Parish of St. Margaret Westminster in the County of London

No.	When married	Name and Surname	Age	Condition	Rank or profession	Residence at the time of marriage	Father's name and surname	Rank or profession of father
483	September 12th 1908	Winston Leonard Spencer Churchill	33	Bachelor	President of Board of Trade	Board of Trade, 7 Whitehall Gardens S.W.	Lord Randolph Churchill (deceased)	M.P. sometime Secretary of State, Chancellor of the Exchequer
	1908	Clementine Ogilvy Hozier	23	Spinster	—	51 Abingdon Villas, Sir Henry Hozier Kensington	(deceased)	Colonel

Married in the Parish Church according to the Rites and Ceremonies of the Established Church by licence by me

Winston Leonard Spencer Churchill   in the   A. G. St Asaph
Clementine Ogilvy Hozier   presence of us,

CERTIFIED to be a true copy of an entry in the certified copy of a Register of Marriages in the District above mentioned.
Given at the GENERAL REGISTER OFFICE, LONDON, under the Seal of the said Office, the 9th day of August 1977.

MB 167904

CAUTION—Any person who (1) falsifies any of the particulars on this certificate, or (2) uses a falsified certificate as true, knowing it to be false, is liable to prosecution.

CERTIFIED COPY OF AN ENTRY OF DEATH   Given at the GENERAL REGISTER OFFICE, LONDON.

Application Number Q·8·D

REGISTRATION DISTRICT Kensington

1965. DEATH in the Sub-district of Kensington South in the Royal Borough of Kensington

No.	When and where died	Name and surname	Sex	Age	Occupation	Cause of death	Signature, description, and residence of informant	When registered	Signature of registrar
10	Twenty fourth January 1965 28 Hyde Park Gate Kensington	Winston Leonard Spencer Churchill	Male	90 years	The Right Honourable K.G. O.M. C.H. Statesman	I(a) Cerebral Thrombosis (b) Cerebral arteriosclerosis II Congestion of lungs Certified by Moran M.R.C.S.	A. A. D. Montague Browne Present at the death 28 Hyde Park Gate S.W.	Twenty Sixth January 1965	Registrar

CERTIFIED to be a true copy of an entry in the certified copy of a Register of Deaths in the District above mentioned.
Given at the GENERAL REGISTER OFFICE, LONDON, under the Seal of the said Office, the 12th day of August 1977.

DA 654825

CAUTION—Any person who (1) falsifies any of the particulars on this certificate, or (2) uses a falsified certificate as true, knowing it to be false, is liable to prosecution.

8

PEDIGREE CHART

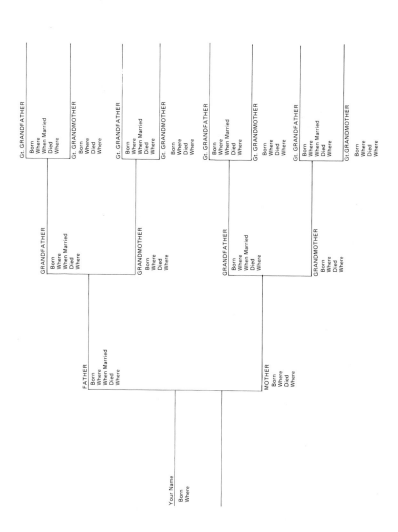

Your Name
Born
Where

FATHER
Born
Where
When Married
Died
Where

MOTHER
Born
Where
Died
Where

GRANDFATHER
Born
Where
When Married
Died
Where

GRANDMOTHER
Born
Where
Died
Where

GRANDFATHER
Born
Where
When Married
Died
Where

GRANDMOTHER
Born
Where
Died
Where

Gt. GRANDFATHER
Born
Where
When Married
Died
Where

Gt. GRANDMOTHER
Born
Where
Died
Where

Gt. GRANDFATHER
Born
Where
When Married
Died
Where

Gt. GRANDMOTHER
Born
Where
Died
Where

Gt. GRANDFATHER
Born
Where
When Married
Died
Where

Gt. GRANDMOTHER
Born
Where
Died
Where

Gt. GRANDFATHER
Born
Where
When Married
Died
Where

Gt.GRANDMOTHER
Born
Where
Died
Where

A NOVEL WAY OF PREPARING YOUR FAMILY TREE

You can extend this circle to include your Gt.Gt. Grand-parents and Gt.Gt.Gt. Grandparents, and so on.

Paternal

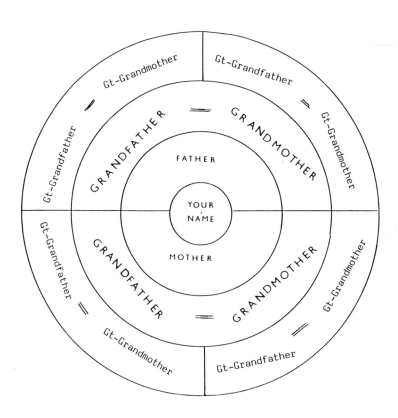

maternal

TYPICAL RECORD SHEET

NAME	FATHER	MOTHER	BORN		DIED		MARRIED			OFF SPRING	
			DATE	PLACE	DATE	PLACE	DATE	PLACE	WHO	M	F

LESSON No. 4

Of the many and varied records available for research the Parish Records are the most important. Before 1st July 1837 the principal means of recording births and/or baptisms, marriages and deaths or burials were these records kept by clergymen of the Church of England, known as Parish Records. The best way to trace such records is to get in touch with the Minister of the Church in which the ceremony is thought to have taken place.

These records go back to 1538 and it was in this year that Thomas Cromwell, as the King's Minister, issued an order that in each Parish in England and Wales the parson, in the presence of the churchwardens, should keep a strict record of all baptisms, marriages and burials during the preceding week, these should be written in a suitable book (known as Parish Records) and locked away for safe keeping. This law was not, however, a very popular one and there was some resistance to its introduction. It was, nevertheless the commencement of the Parish Registers. In the mid 16th century an order was passed for transcripts to be made from these early registers within a month after Easter for the Previous year for submission to the Bishop's Registrar. These transcripts are known as Bishop's Transcripts and are now normally deposited in your local **DRO** (Diocesan Record Office) or the archives section of your reference library.

In 1754 a further Act was introduced by Lord Hardwicke and called Hardwicke's Marriage Act, this introduced a separate register for marriages and details had to be entered on printed forms which had to be signed by the officiating minister, the bride and groom and two witnesses. This Act also stipulated that, before a marriage could be performed it had to be preceded by the calling of banns for three successive weeks in the Parish Church of both the bride and groom. The only way round this was to apply to the church authorities for a special licence, this was granted under special circumstances. This Act exempts Quakers and Jews as their records were considered satisfactory.

Careful perusal of these records is necessary and with patience your efforts will be rewarded. Many of these P.R's are in your local DRO or Reference Library, quite a few are on micro-film. When making your research keep a strict record of all entries relating to the name you are researching for these may be Gt. Aunts and Uncles that you did not know existed.

The Church of Jesus Christ of Latter Day Saints, commonly known as Mormons, have computer files recording of entries from Parish Registers from all over the world. These relate to baptisms and marriages only. They record surnames in alphabetical order for specific areas i.e. counties. All these records are on Microfiche and can be viewed at your local DRO or Reference Library or at the local Mormon Church. These are known as the International Genealogical Index (IGI). The originals are housed in mountain vaults in Salt Lake City, Utah, U.S.A. These are a great help when undertaking family research. The index contains over 66 million names from the early 1500s to about 1870. Areas covered include Scotland, Wales, Ireland, Scandinavian and European countries and over 70 other countries. These indexes are periodically updated, the latest issue being 1988. Over 60% of English Parishes have been filmed. Some CRO's and DRO's have the complete indexes for Great Britain. They are mainly Church of England records, Roman Catholic and nonconformist records have NOT been included, these can be seen in local parish churches and in some DRO's.

In 1851, in addition to the census of population, a census was taken of places of worship. Although this was purely voluntary, most places of worship made returns. These returns for England and Wales are now among the Home Office records in the Public Record Office (HO 129), which may be seen only at the PRO, Ruskin Avenue, KEW. These returns show the name and denomination of each place of worship, including those of Roman Catholic and dissenting Protestant congregations, the date of consecration or erection and the space available for public worship. They also give records of attendances at the various services on 30 March 1851, and average attendances for the previous year. They often include information about buildings and endowments and comments by the Minister. These returns are arranged by registration districts.

SUITABLE REFERENCE BOOKS:—

Crockfords Clerical Directory.
Boyd's Marriage Index.
* Phillimore Atlas & Index of Parish Registers.
* Tracing your Ancestors in the Public Record Office
    by Jane Cox & Timothy Padfield.
* In search of Scottish Ancestry
    by G. Hamilton-Edwards.
* In Search of Welsh Ancestry
    by G. Hamilton-Edwards.
* Irish Genealogy: A Record Finder
    by D.F. Begley.

* If any of these publications are NOT in your Public Library or Local Bookshop they can be purchased direct from the Society of Genealogists in London.

MICROFICHE

This is a section of a microfiche page of the I.G.I. (International Genealogical Index) which is referred to in lesson No. 4.

COUNTRY: ENGLAND COUNTY: YORK AS OF JUN 1981

NAME	SEX	FATHER, MOTHER OR SPOUSE	TYPE	EVENT DATE	TOWN, PARISH
LITCHFIELD, JAMES	M	ANN NOE	M	14APR1800	ROTHERHAM
LITCHFIELD, JAMES	M	WILLIAM LICHFIELD/SARAH	C	22MAY1831	WORSBOROUGH
LITCHFIELD, JOHN	M	HANNAH FRYER	M	03JUN1683	BRAMHAM
LIECHFEILD, JOHN	M	SARAH LAMBERT	M	08MAY1698	ROTHERHAM
LITCHFIELD, JOHN	M	JAMES LITCHFIELD/ANN	C	23FEB1817	WENTWORTH
LITCHFIELD, JOHN EDWIN	M	JOHN LITCHFIELD/HANNAH	C	16APR1843	WENTWORTH
LICHFIELD, JOSEPH	M	MATTHEW LICHFIELD/MARY	C	23FEB1834	WENTWORTH
LICHFIELD, LOUISA	F	WILLIAM LICHFIELD/SARAH	C	30AUG1829	WENTWORTH
LITCHFIELD, LUCY	F	WILLIAM LITCHFIELD/SARAH	C	27AUG1826	WENTWORTH
LITCHFIELD, LUCY	F	WILLIAM LITCHFIELD/SARAH	C	24DEC1826	WENTWORTH
LITCHFIELD, MARTHA	F	CHARLES ROODHOUSE	M	25OCT1830	ROTHERHAM
LITCHFIELD, MARTHA	F	WILLIAM LITCHFIELD/SARAH	C	07APR1833	WORSBOROUGH
LICHFIELD, MARY	F		C	17SEP1843	PENISTONE
LITCHFIELD, MATTHEW	M	GEORGE LICHFIELD/SARAH KENWORTHY MARY ELLIS	M	01MAR1830	WATH UPON DEARNE
LETCHFIELD, SALLY	F	WILLIAM LETCHFIELD/MARY	C	08MAY1823	BULMER
LITCHFIELD, SARAH	F	MATTHEW LITCHFIELD/MARY	C	02APR1837	WENTWORTH
LICHFIELD, THOMAS	M	JAMES LICHFIELD/ANN	C	12AUG1814	WENTWORTH
LICHFIELD, THOMAS	M	MATTHEW LICHFIELD/MARY	C	06MAR1831	WENTWORTH
LITCHFIELD, THOMAS	M	WILLIAM LITCHFIELD/SARAH	C	26JUL1835	WORSBOROUGH
LETCHFIELD, WILLIAM	M	WILLIAM LETCHFIELD/MARY	M	20MAR1821	BULMER
LITCHFIELD, WILLIA?	M	SARAH PICKERING	M	09OCT1825	ROTHERHAM
LITCHFIELD, WILLIA?	M	JOHN LITCHFIELD/HANNAH	C	19APR1841	WENTWORTH
LITCHIN — LETCHEN, WILLIAM	M	JOHN LETCHEN/MARY BRIGGS	C	31AUG1794	YORK, SAINT MARY CASTLE
LITCHMAN — LITCHMAN, FRANCES LEONORA	F	JOHN LITCHMAN/HANNAH BUSSEY	C	22OCT1793	YORK, SAINT MARTIN AND

LESSON No. 5

CENSUS RETURNS

Since the year 1801 a regular census of the population has taken place every 10 years, this covered England and Wales, Isle of Man and the Channel Isles. The returns up to 1841 are of little use to the family historian as the names of the residents were not recorded. These were taken in 1841 on the 7th June. These returns are not available for public inspection until they are 100 years old. The origianl returns are held at the Public Record Office, Portugal Street, London (see map) and they are on micro film for public inspection. Certain DRO's and Reference Libraries do have copies appertaining to their areas. Details of this year of census includes, full name; age, sex; and occupation. The ages of individuals under 15 years are given exactly; the ages of others were rounded down to the nearest 5 years, for example a person actually aged 64 appears as 60, another aged 29 appears as 25. The relationship between members of a single household are not recorded but can usually be inferred. Information about place of birth is restricted to whether or not an individual was born in the county of residence, and if not, whether in Scotland (S), Ireland (I) or Foreign Parts (F).

Censuses of 1851 to 1881. These returns were taken on 30 March 1851, 7 April 1861, 2 April 1871 and the 3 April 1881, give full name; exact age; relationship to the head (H) of the household; sex; occupation; and parish and county of birth. There was no census taken in 1941.

The census room is open between 9.30 am to 4.50 pm on weekdays only.

Owing to the topographical arrangements of these

returns it is *essential to know at least the approximate address, at the time of the census,* of the person or persons whose names are sought, before any search becomes practicable.

If you cannot attend personally write for an application form, then limited searches will be made by the staff, in return for a fee.

The returns of the censuses for the years 1891 and 1901 for the mentioned areas are in the custody of the Registrar General and are closed to general inspection for 100 years. The Registrar General will, however, supply to direct descendants only, and in exchange for a fee, the age and place of birth of named persons to whom a precise address can be given. Application should be sent to:-

Registrar General,
Office of Population Censuses and Surveys,
St. Catherines House,
Kingsway, London WC2B 6JP.

Surviving returns for Scotland are held in:-

The General Register Office,
New Register House,
Edinburgh. EH1 3YT.

No census returns for Ireland earlier than 1901 and 1911 have survived. Returns of these censuses for the whole of Ireland are available in:-

Public Record Office of Ireland,
Four Courts,
Dublin, Ireland.

If you make a personal visit to the **PRO** arm yourself with a pencil (pens are **NOT** allowed).

17

LESSON No. 6

WILLS and ADMINISTRATION ORDERS

A Will is a personal document left by the deceased and give the family historian much valuable information once traced i.e. names of relatives and family, details of property owned, assets and sometimes the occupation of the deceased.

The Court of Probate Act 1857 came into effect on the 12th January 1858 and since that date wills proved in England and Wales have been maintained at the Principal Registry of the Family Division, Somerset House, Strand, London WC2R 1LP. The indexes are in the form of yearly volumes and can be consulted free of charge. When you have found the entry you require, you have to take the volume to the clerk at the reception desk, who then enters the details on the appropriate form and a search is then made for the copy will. This usually takes about 15 minutes. You can then view the copy for 25p and you are allowed to make notes from the contents.

If you require a copy of the will this will cost you 25p per page, this will be taken and posted to you within 7 to 10 days. It is well to remember that a copy will be much cheaper than a copy death certificate. Some Local Reference Libraries and CRO's have copies of local wills covering their area.

In cases where no will was made, letters of administration (abbreviated-admonds) were granted to the next-of-kin, giving him/her the authority to distribute the intestate's estate. The indexes of these too can be viewed in this section.

Prior to the 12th January 1858 the wills proved in the senior probate court, the Prerogative Court of Canterbury (known as PCC) are held at the Public Record Office, Chancery Lane, London, these cover the period 1384 to 1858. If you wish, you can write and ask them to make

18

a search of a will for you, covering a period of three years from the date of death.   If they are successful they will send you an estimate of the cost of supplying photo-copies.   The records of other courts are preserved locally and you should contact your local **DRO** for information. Details of these records are given in two publications, a copy of which can be seen in your **DRO** or Reference Library:-

Wills and their Whereabouts by Anthony J. Camp.
and Wills and Where to find them by J.S.W. Gibson.

ESTATE DUTY REGISTERS

Legacy or death duty was first introduced from 1796 to 1894, this made tax payable on the estate of deceased persons.   The registers and their indexes can be inspected at the **PRO** in London.   The information obtained can be an aid to the whereabouts of a will for it gives details of the Court in which the will was proven or an admond granted.   It also gives the name of legatees and their degree of consanguinity, names and addresses and occu-pation of the executors.   A hive of information for the researcher.

DIVORCE PROCEEDINGS

Owing to the sharp increase in divorce it may be necessary to apply for a copy of a decree absolute in certain circumstances.   You have to apply to the Divorce Registry, Room G45, Somerset House, Strand, London WC2R 1LP.   You can make a personal application or by post.   Forward a cheque or postal order for £2.00 made payable to H.M. PAYMASTER GENERAL and crossed & Co.   The details they require are as follows:-
1. Full names of the Petitioner in the case (the party who began proceedings).
2. Full names of the Respondent spouse.
3. Full names of the Co-Respondent (if any) or any other party THIS IS MOST IMPORTANT.
4. (a) Date of marriage (b) Date of separation.
5. The date on or year in which the Petition was filed, and in which Registry it was filed.
6. The date on or year in which the decree nisi was pronounced and the Court.
7. The date on or year in which the decree nisi was made absolute.
Applicant's Name and Address.

LAND and MANORIAL ROLLS

These can be a valuable source of information in your research into your family history for, if you can identify the Manor in which your ancestor lived, the perusal of Title Deeds, Hearth Tax Returns, Enclosure Awards and Tithe Records can yield details of the mode of living of the occupants at that time. These documents can be found in CRO's, and at the PRO in London. The British Library in Great Russell Street, London WC1 is a valuable source for manuscript information, however, admission to the Reference Division of this library is subject to proof of an intention to carry out research, or reference work which cannot reasonably be carried out in another library. Admission is by *reader's pass only*, write and ask them to forward form RD/RAB for completion.

BURGESS ROLLS

The Burgess Rolls originated during the reign of HENRY VIII and are a veritable mine of information for the researcher. Each burgess on enrolment had to give his full name, profession and address of his father and himself together with the names and ages of all his children then living. This gave you three generations of a family in one entry. Admission as a burgess could only be obtained (1) by birth in the town (2) by descent from a burgess (3) by serving as apprentice to a burgess (4) by purchase.
The Rights and Privileges of a burgess were as follows:-

(1) Right to trade in the town. (2) Free education for his sons. (3) Entitlement to vote at elections.

During the 17th century it became the common custom to admit a man as a burgess together with any of his sons who were then living, some were quite young children. The father paid their fee, (this was usually £5.00 but a gentleman paid double) together with his own but they were only 'admitted', they had to be sworn as burgess when they reached the age of 21. If a man could prove that his father had been a 'Burgess by descent' he could not, however, exercise the rights of a burgess until he was sworn in at 21. These rolls can normally be viewed at CRO or DRO's but it must be pointed out that many over the years have been lost or destroyed.

POLL BOOKS and VOTERS LISTS

A brief history of the Franchise and Registration of Electors reveals that in 1429, (the 15th Century) the qualification for the county franchise was the possession of freehold property of annual value of 40/-. The proportion of electorate to population was 1 in 50. This remained unaltered until 1832 when it was extended to the owners of all property and to occupiers of property rented at £50 or more. The borough franchise was extended to occupiers of property to the value of £10. At this stage the Register of Electors was established and the proportion of electorate to population was increased to 1 in 24.

In 1884 a further act was passed, sometimes called the Gladstone's Act, this reduced the proportion of electorate to 1 in 6. In 1918 yet another act was passed extending franchise to all men over 21 years of age to residential qualifications; to women over 30 years of age subject to the prescribed qualifications. This now reduced the proportion of electorate to 1 in 3½. Several other acts were implemented but it was not until 1945 - 1948 that Registers were compiled on the basis of National Registration records plus service or business premises voters and ratepayers votes. Each voter had now to qualify on his or her own right. In 1969 the voting age from 21 years to 18 years of age was introduced. What a hive of information for the family historian! Poll books and Voters lists can be viewed at Reference Libraries, CRO's and DRO's.

MONUMENTAL INSCRIPTIONS

The Federation of Family History Societies has a long term plan to record the monumental inscriptions in all the churches and churchyards throughout the country. There are over 70 Family History and Genealogical Societies in Great Britain and, members of these, for many years now have been researching churchyards in their areas and recording full details of burials, these have been recorded and published, (sometimes microfiched) in order to help with this plan. These recordings are retained by each society but copies have been deposited in local Reference Libraries and CRO's and in The Society of Genealogists in London. These can be a great help in your research. If you wish to research Public Cemeteries and Crematoriums you should contact the Environment Services Department in your Local Authority.

PUBLIC RECORD OFFICE

The PRO holds records of the government and the central law courts from the eleventh century. It has two main repositories, Chancery Lane in London and Ruskin Avenue in Kew, Richmond, Surrey (see maps).

Offices are open from 9.30 am to 5.00 pm Monday to Friday. When making a written application you must indicate just what you are researching. THEY WILL THEN ADVISE YOU WHICH PRO to attend.

Please note that if you decide to visit Public Record Offices you will need to obtain a reader's ticket. To do this, please bring with you on your first visit some documentary proof of identity. If you are a citizen of the United Kingdom or the Republic of Ireland, a driving licence or banker's card will constitute suitable identification. If you are a citizen of any other country, you will be required to produce your passport.

PHOTOGRAPHIC RECORDS

When visiting your ancestral areas why not take photographs in the location visited; a photograph of your Grandparents home, (if still standing) or the church in which they got married or baptised! What a bonus for your records. An instamatic camera is sufficient for outdoor shots on a bright fine day but, for perfection I recommend a 35mm camera using a 400ASA film. You can purchase these in black and white or colour. This will ensure a good photograph under adverse weather conditions.

CONCLUSION

I do hope that, after studying these lessons, that your interest in tracing your family tree has been enhanced. It is a very time consuming but interesting hobby.

When compiling your tree in the standard form, as stated in Lessons 1, 2, 3, you can also research and enter the marriages of your other relations, this will then finally complete your family tree. In all your subjects, you could add additional details i.e. after the born date, enter the area in which born and, after the father's name, state his occupation.

VJP

INFORMATION SECTION

DIOCESE RECORD OFFICE (DRO)

In addition to the Record Offices there are other sources from which useful information can be obtained which will be helpful in your research especially the DRO's and the Archives Section of Reference Libraries. In addition to having copies on microfilm of the local census returns they have copies of Parish Registers, Bishops Transcripts, Local Wills, Burgess and Voters Lists, old and modern directories, maps showing diocese areas etc. The following list of such offices and libraries may be of assistance:-

ENGLAND

BIRMINGHAM	Reference Library, Chamberlain Square, B3 3HQ
	Midland Institute Library, Margaret Street, B3 (This is for members only)
BRADFORD	Archives Dept. Central Library, Princes Way, BD1 1NN.
BRISTOL	City Archivist, The Council House, College Green, BS1 5TR
CANTERBURY	The Precincts, Kent. CT1 2EG
COVENTRY	Broadgate House, Broadgate.
HEREFORD	Broad Street, Hereford & Worcester. HR4 9AU
HULL	Guildhall, Kingston upon Hull, North Humberside. HU1 2AA.
LEEDS	Chapeltown Road, Sheepscar, LS7 3AP
MANCHESTER	St. Peter's Square, M2 5PD
NOTTINGHAM	South Sherwood Street.
OXFORD	Bodleian Library, OX1 3BG
ROCHESTER	The Precincts, Kent.
SALISBURY	The Wren Hall, The Close, Wiltshire.
SHEFFIELD	Surrey Street, S1 1XZ

SHREWSBURY   St. Mary's Hall, St. Mary's Place, SY1 1DZ.

STAFFORD   William Salt Library, Eastgate Street, ST16 2IZ (This is adjacent to the RO)

SOUTHAMPTON Civic Centre, SO9 4XL

YORK   Borthwick Institute, St. Anthony's Hall, Yorks. YO1 2OW.

WALES

National Library of Wales, ABERYSTWYTH, Dyfed SY23 3BU

Glamorgan Archive Service, County Hall, Cathays Park, CARDIFF, CF1 3NE

Gwynedd Archives Service. Cae Penarlag, DOLGELLAU, Gwynedd.

ISLE OF MAN

Civil registration of marriages started in 1849, and of births and deaths in 1878. The records are held by the Island's General Registry, Finch Road, Douglas. Wills are also kept in the General Registry.

CHANNEL ISLANDS

Civil registration of births and deaths started in 1840 and of marriages in 1919. For these records and also wills application should be made to the Judical Greffe at The States' Building, Royal Square, St. Helier, Jersey. C.I. or to the Royal Court House, St. Peter Port, Guernsey, C.I.

DISTRICT PROBATE REGISTRIES

BIRMINGHAM   Cavendish House, Waterloo Street, B2 5PS.

BRIGHTON   28 Richmond Place, BN2 2NA.

BRISTOL   4th Floor, 37-41 Prince Street, BS1 4PX.

IPSWICH   15 Museum Street, IP1 1HG.

LEEDS   Devereux House, East Parade, LS1 2BA.

Wills are only retained at these registeries for the past 50 years.

MILITARY RECORDS

These are held at the PRO in Kew, Richmond, Surrey. (see map page 30 and see note on page 33).

COLLEGE OF ARMS

Queen Victoria Street, London EC4V 4BT. Tel: 01 248 2762.   If the family name you are researching is thought to have a coat of arms, information concerning it can be obtained from this College which is the official repository in England of records of Coat of Arms.   The heralds, over the past four centuries, have also recorded pedigrees, both in connection with proof of a right to arms and for purely genealogical interest, and this continues.   The heralds can make searches in their records and will also undertake genealogical research in the national and local records outside the College, for this a fee is charged.   The Officer in Waiting will be glad to advise and assist.

Royal Coat of Arms.

SCOTLAND, IRELAND AND THE IRISH REPUBLIC

Postal applications for certificates of events which occurred in Scotland, Northern Ireland and the Irish Republic.

The Registrar General, New Register House, Edinburgh EH1 3YT. Edinburgh (031) 556 3952 Ext. 64

Short (abbreviated) certificate of birth £2.50

Full certificate of birth, death or marriage £5.00

Second or any subsequent extract of the same entry issued at the same time £2.50

Where a search is made and the entry is not found, a fee of £2.50 is chargeable for each period of five years or part thereof searched.

The Registrar General, Oxford House, 49/55 Chichester Street, Belfast. BT1 4HL. Belfast (0232) 235211.

Short certificate of birth £2.25

Full certificate of birth, death or marriage . . . . £3.75 (including 5 year search fee of £1.25)

When applying by post, applicants are advised to remit an amount sufficient to cover both the search fee and the certificate fee.

The Registrar General, Joyce House, 8/11 Lombard St. East, Dublin 2. Dublin (0001) 711000

Short certificate of birth £1.50

Full certificate of birth, death or marriage £3.00

Any enquiries about the fees set out above should be addressed to Edinburgh, Belfast or Dublin, as appropriate.

GENERAL REGISTRATION REGIONS: 1837-51

I	West London
II	East London
III	Middlesex
IV	Surrey
V	Kent
VI	Bedfordshire, Berkshire (part of), Buckinghamshire, Hertfordshire
VII	Hampshire (part of), Sussex
VIII	Dorset, Hampshire (part of), Wiltshire
IX	Cornwall, Scilly Isles, Devon (part of)
X	Devon (part of), Somerset (part of)
XI	Gloucestershire (part of), Somerset (part of)
XII	Essex, Suffolk (part of)
XIII	Norfolk, Suffolk (part of)
XIV	Cambridgeshire, Huntingdonshire, Lincolnshire
XV	Leicestershire, Northamptonshire Nottinghamshire, Rutland
XVI	Berkshire (part of), Oxfordshire, Staffordshire (part of), Warwickshire (part of)
XVII	Staffordshire (part of)
XVIII	Gloucestershire (part of), Shropshire Staffordshire (part of), Warwickshire (part of), Worcestershire
XIX	Cheshire, Derbyshire, Flintshire (part of)
XX	Lancashire (part of)
XXI	Lancashire (part of, Yorkshire (part of)
XXII	West Riding (part of), East Riding (part of)
XXIII	West Riding (part of), East Riding (part of)
XXIV	County Durham, North Riding
XXV	Cumberland, Lancashire (part of), Northumberland, Westmorland
XXVI	South Wales, Herefordshire
XXVII	North Wales, Anglesey

27

GENERAL REGISTRATION REGIONS: 1852-1946
(August)

1a - 1d	Greater London
2a	Surrey, Kent
2b - 2c	Sussex, Hampshire (part of)
2d	Berkshire, Hampshire (part of)
3a	Middlesex, Hertfordshire, Oxfordshire, Buckinghamshire
3b	Bedfordshire, Cambridgeshire, Huntingdonshire, Northamptonshire
4a	Essex, Suffolk
4b	Norfolk
5a	Wiltshire, Dorset
5b	Devon
5c	Cornwall, Scilly Isles, Somerset
6a	Gloucestershire, Herefordshire, Shropshire
6b	Staffordshire, Warwickshire (part of) Worcestershire (part of)
6c	Warwickshire (part of), Worcestershire (part of)
6d	Warwickshire (part of)
7a	Leicestershire, Lincolnshire, Rutland
7b	Derbyshire, Nottinghamshire
8a	Cheshire
8b - 8e	Lancashire
9a - 9d	Yorkshire
10a	County Durham
10b	Cumberland, Northumberland, Westmorland
11a	South Coast Wales
11b	North Wales, Anglesey

These numbers are stated in the index which you are researching in St. Catherine's House in London, under Vol. No., and, as you can see, these indicate the county in which the entry is recorded. This will be helpful to you, if you know the county in which your ancestor was at that particular period.

SOCIETY OF GENEALOGISTS

Society of Genealogists, 14 Charterhouse Buildings, Goswell Road, London EC1M 7BA. Tel: 01 251 8799.

This Society was founded in 1911 to promote and encourage the study of genealogy and heraldry. Subscription Rates for Members. There is an entrance fee when first joining of £7.50. The annual subscription for those living within 25 miles from Trafalgar Square in London is £25.00. For those living outside this limit it is £16.00. Subscriptions are due on the 1st January. Search Fees for Non-Members. These may use the Library on payment of fees for 1 hour £2.50, Half Day £6.00, Full Day £8.00. You must enclose a s.a.e. when writing for information.

Their library has the largest collection of Parish Registers copies in the country around 8000 mostly from the sixteenth century to 1812. Others up to 1837 or later, these are Church of England registers but the collection also includes over 600 non-conformist registers as well. A visit to this Society is recommended.

LOCAL HISTORY and or GENEALOGICAL SOCIETIES

As previously stated, there are over 70 of these societies in Great Britain and, I would advise you to join your local society, the name and address can be obtained from your local library. Monthly meetings are arranged, talks given, also outings to places of interest, you will also make many new friends. For example the Birmingham and Midland Society for Genealogy and Heraldry, which was founded in 1963, have branches in Burton on Trent, North Staffs, Kenilworth and District, Stourbridge and District, Wolverhampton and District & Worcester Branch. I suggest that you write to The Secretary, Mrs. June Watkins, 92 Dimmingsdale Bank, Birmingham B32 1ST for details.

STAFFORDSHIRE PARISH REGISTERS SOCIETY

This Society was founded on the 16th January 1900. The Bishop of Lichfield proposed that a society be formed to print Parish Registers and the motion was seconded and carried. Lord Dartmouth was appointed President of the Society and Sir Reginald Hardy became Hon. Secretary.

Since then the Society has published over 90 registers covering the Staffordshire area. They may have the one you require in your family research.

Current membership costs only £2.00 p.a. and each member receives a free copy of a register as soon as it is published.   Application for information and/or membership should be sent to A.T.C. Lavender, Hon. Secretary and Treasurer, 91 Brenton Road, Penn, Wolverhampton, West Midlands. WV4 5NS.

When writing to any of the addresses given in this book you must enclose a stamped addressed envelope for a reply.

PUBLIC RECORDS OFFICE

KEW
RICHMOND
SURREY
TW9 4DU
Telephone: 01 876 3444

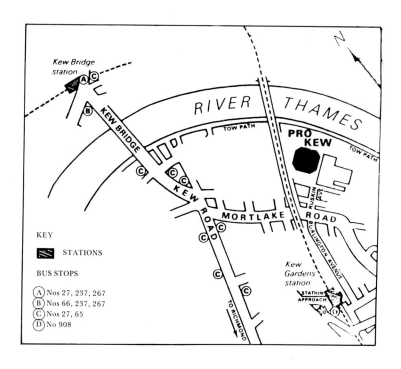

THE RESEARCH AREA IN LONDON

Map of the research area in London

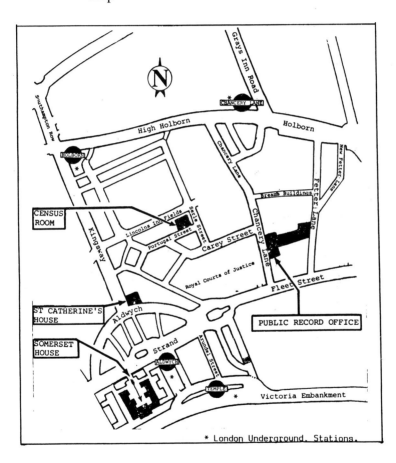

Telephone Numbers:—
PUBLIC RECORD OFFICE   01 876 3444
St. Catherine's House   01 242 0262 Ex. 2051
Census Room (PRO)   01 405 3488
Somerset House   01 936 6947

SOCIETY OF GENEALOGISTS – LOCATION

How to find the Society of Genealogists
14, Charterhouse Buildings, Goswell Road,
LONDON EC1 7BA.

The Society's rooms are situated in a cul-de-sac at the junction of Goswell Road and Clerkenwell Road, about 500 yards north of Barbican Station, which is on the Circle and Metropolitan Underground lines. Buses, Nos 4, 5 and 55, stop nearby.

Being close to the City, the Society's Library is conveniently situated for use in conjunction with many record repositories in London.

Tel: 01 251 8799

From most London railway termini - Circle Line to Barbican Underground Station.

From Waterloo Station - Nos 4 or 5 buses direct; or Underground to Embankment and Circle Line to Barbican Underground Station.

From London Bridge Station - Underground to Moorgate and Circle Line to Barbican Underground Station.

From Aldwych - No 4 bus, along Fleet Street, or No 5 bus up Kingsway.

If you wish to make enquiries concerning members of your family who served in the Armed Services, you should contact the following establishments:-

ROYAL NAVY
Ministry of Defence CS(R)2a, Bourne Avenue, Hayes, Middlesex UB3 1 RF.
This department holds service records of non-commissioned ranks dating from 1892 to 1929. Post 1929 records are held at:-

D/NPP (ACS) 3B(IV), HMS Centurion, Grange Road, Gosport, Hants. PO13 9XA.

Enquiries concerning Officers and its reserve branches from circa 1890 should be addressed to:-

The Naval Secretary, Room 110, Ripley Block, Old Admiralty Building, Spring Gardens, London SW1A 2BE.

ROYAL MARINES
Drafting and Record Office Royal Marines, HMS Centurion, Grange Road, Gosport, Hants. PO13 9XA.

This department holds records of RM who enlisted since 1925.

ARMY
Ministry of Defence, Army Record Centre, Bourne Avenue, Hayes, Middlesex. UB3 1RF.

This department hold all surviving records for those who served in the Army from the outbreak of the First World War up until 1980.

Records prior to the mentioned dates given above are held at the PRO in Kew.

ROYAL AIR FORCE
Ministry of Defence, Royal Air Force Personnel Management Centre, Eastern Avenue, Gloucester GL4 7PN.

ANNIVERSARIES AND BIRTHSTONES

As we are dealing with years and months during our family research, the following may be of an added interest.

WEDDING ANNIVERSARIES are named as follows:-

1st.	Cotton	13th.	Lace
2nd.	Paper	14th.	Ivory
3rd.	Leather	15th.	Crystal
4th.	Fruit	20th.	China
5th.	Wooden	25th.	Silver
6th.	Sugar	30th.	Pearl
7th.	Wool	40th.	Ruby
8th.	Bronze	45th.	Sapphire
9th.	Pottery	50th.	Golden
10th.	Tin	55th.	Emerald
11th.	Steel	60th.	Diamond
12th.	Silk	70th.	Platinum

BIRTH STONES

January	Garnet	July	Ruby
February	Amethyst	August	Sardonyx
March	Bloodstone	September	Sapphire
April	Diamond	October	Opal
May	Emerald	November	Topaz
June	Pearl	December	Turquoise.